D0457151

# Japanese
# TANKA

*The Court Poetry of a Golden Age*

By Thomas Gurgal, with
Illustrations by Maggie Jarvis

## The Peter Pauper Press

Mount Vernon, New York

# Introduction

THE *tanka*, with its thirty-one syllables arranged in lines of 5, 7, 5, 7 and 7, is the aboriginal form of Japanese poetry. *Tanka* were recited before Japan had a written language and are still composed today. The great poem contest held in Japan each year under the sponsorship of the Emperor is limited to *tanka*.

The *tanka* had its greatest vogue in the tenth, eleventh and twelfth centuries, during the Heian period, Japan's golden age. The form calls up a vision of a languid lady in a palace lined with screens and colorful sliding walls, reading the thirty-one syllable statement of the heart of some moody nobleman and answering that missive in another thirty-one syllables in tasteful imagery and elegant calligraphy. It was the Heian greeting card, and it is today, in Japan as elsewhere, an apt medium for sentiments passionate or delicate.

ALFRED H. MARKS
Editor-in-Chief, *Literature East & West*

# Preface

IF this volume is a positive reflection on the art of poetry and the art of tanka, I owe credit to several people. While a student, I was struck by one of the well aimed arrows of Professor Alfred H. Marks, renowned translator and dynamic scholar; he taught me the rules of form and shades of word play that characterize Japanese poetry and the tanka in particular. Through him I met the tuberculine ghost of Japan's Virgil: Ishikawa Takuboku who, by twisting the shaft, taught me image.

It was not, however, until a girl, fresh with the playfulness of youth, plucked a few of her hairs to give me, as though they were flowers, that this book began to write itself. Although my rough lines are only a first step, the tanka is as old as Japanese culture and well deserves the enduring honor time has bestowed on it. If the reader balks at its limitation of five lines and thirty-one syllables, I have included a poem by Yosano Akiko, outspoken poetess of modern Japan, giving sharp defense of this brief but

venerable form. Here I have only this to add
concerning tanka in English:

> *When a cherry sprig*
> *Grafted to an apple bough*
> *Bears us fuller fruit,*
> *Who would thus be brash enough*
> *To call them less than apples?*

T. G.

# Japanese Tanka

# Japanese
## Tanka

To Jan

Like empty cocoons
When the butterfly has flown
Words are hollow shells.
Why should I embrace the husk
When the wheat is full and golden?


To Takuboku

You give me your toys;
Over my trembling fingers
You cast silver spells.
Now I can feel your dark gaze
Dark in whispering shadows.

I come here again
   To the changeless countryside
      Of my lost youth.
         I come to visit the lone grave,
            This, the grave of my first love.

                                    ISHIKAWA TAKUBOKU


The sun is setting;
   Clouds drift aimlessly across
      This face of the moon.
         Motionless I watch and watch;
            What do they matter to me?

                                    ISHIKAWA TAKUBOKU


When the dew gathers
   On these lespedeza leaves,
      They must feel chilly.
         On this windy Autumn moor,
            Even the deer are crying.

                                    LADY SAGAMI

10

O, my gem-strung soul,

   If you must snap, snap now;

      To endure the dawn,

         Hostile eyes would surely pierce

         Into this my aching love.

PRINCESS SHIKESHI

Hey there traveler!

How cold your sleeves have become;

How this bay wind blows,

Pushing past bleak Suma —

Barrier to old friendships.

ARIWARA YUKIHIRA

*(exiled to this remote island noted for
salt marshes and forbidding reefs)*

This Autumn evening,

With mists trailing through the trees

On Cypress Mountain,

One cannot ask loneliness

Of its birthplace or parents.

PRIEST JAKUREN

Rather than worry,

Uselessly, like a miser

Over his dead gold,

One should drink down this Jewel —

One cup of rough wrought saki.

OTOMO TABITO

12

At Iwashiro,

    I bind pine branches for luck.

        If charms can change fate,

            I may well return this way

                To thank you friendly shore pine.

                        PRINCE ARIMA


Once I was a prince;

    Now I use grass for pillow

        And eat rice off leaves.

            At home they would serve my food

                From those gilded plates and bowls.

                        PRINCE ARIMA

                    *(exiled and subsequently*
                    *executed at 18 years of age)*


I know what I'd be,

    If I could be other than

        A holy madman.

            I'd be a warm saki cup

                Soaking up warm saki.

                        OTOMO TABITO

At Nigitazu,

    The moon launches our vessels.

        Why do you wonder?

            Moonrise arouses the tide!

                Unfurl your sails and embark!

                            PRINCESS NUKADA


Over lake Omi,

    I hear the plovers crying.

        My heart flies with them

            Over the waves of sunset

                Back to the days of my youth.

                          KAKINOMOTO HITOMARO

Clustered naked men

Starkly stand against the sun;

Great singing hammers

Swing and smash these unwrought rocks—

Metal fragments into time!

TACHIBANA AKEMI

I

Yes my songs are brief;

You think I hoard words meanly,

But I spare nothing.

Unlike fish always puffing,

My soul sings all on one breath.

YOSANO AKIKO

II

Though my skin is soft,

And my veins surge with hot blood,

You never touch me.

Is the Way so exciting

That you must expound always?

YOSANO AKIKO

15

### III

Spring so very short?
  Would you have her immortal
    And thus unchanging?
      With these mortal hands I grope
        For my full and fragrant breasts.

YOSANO AKIKO

### IV

Keep your camellias
  And those pretty plum blossoms;
    They don't become me.
      Peach alone has a color
        That does not ask of my sins.

YOSANO AKIKO

I threw him in chains;
  Locked him in a heavy chest
    And tossed away the key.
      But love, that dauntless scoundrel,
        Has caught up with me once more.

PRINCE HOZUMI

Among you dandies,
  If any should ask about me,
    Here by Suma bay,
      Know that these salty sleeves drip:
        They drip my grieving answer.

ARIWARA YUKIHIRA


You Bodhisattva,
  Earth is redeemed by your smile.
    God may be asleep,
      But if He is dreaming you,
        May He dream eternally.


While in my prison,
  Swallow's soft song touched my heart;
    Was it chance or choice
      That I turned to find your face?
        All day that sun rose and rose.

18

You were all aglow

  When you flew to me last night;

    All that I could do:

      Marvel at your radiance —

        Saw the sun when there was none.

19

## On Seeing Her Scarf

In a sunlit stream
  Sequoias' shade caressing
    The nudity I thumb
      At raging intolerance —
        Scented scarfs unnerve me now?


Go ahead breathe deep;
  No one can see you in here,
    In this catacomb.
      That scarf belongs to a goddess
        Come down on a rainbow bridge.


Entered Autumn's heart;
  Met a rainbow's lovely girl,
    But oh, my stomach! —
      Wriggles like a dying fish
        For want of words to tell her.

20

I write now in fits

   That stalk my old composure;

      Though there is no moon,

         My inner eye sees it shine

           Through walls of apprehension.

21

Can it be my fate?
   I try to resist it so . . .
      Why do I love her?
         Summer wind through summer grasses:
            Softly her voice through my soul.


Happy and so sad;
   Impossibly they tear me
      In two directions;
         The past hangs like a dead skin;
            Your face is all before me.


Stretched and strained my back —
   Like chains my very muscles;
      Pain on pain on pain,
         But I couldn't shake the joy
            That came on yesterday's dream.

All I do is write;

  Love speaks for the silent weeks.

    Now what do I do?

      Breathe joy into slush and snow

        A stranger still to my love?


Time is running out!

  Winter wind grab my collar;

  Sweep me down the street —

    Many worries all about;

      Chance, you must make sure we meet.


I must arise now:

  Must meet my fate face to face.

    Outside on the street,

      Slush and snow mar my way;

        Blue panes reflect a blue sky.

*Teika's holograph: three poems from the poet's own copy of the
personal collection of his pupil Minamoto Sanetomo*

Love or illusion?
 And if love, what can I do
  Not to hurt anyone?
   This is what I think about
    Watching the cloudless blue on blue.


What am I eating?
 Looks like wind swept mountain snow;
  Taste of dry coconut,
   Sickly and without substance.
    In love who needs food anyhow?


All these leftovers —
 Not everyone is in love;
  Don't they understand
   That good form needs content too? —
    The touch of her in passing.

25

Sitting here again —
    These clank and clatter people
    And the singing sky.
        What to do about it all?
            Drink orange juice and whistle.


High mountain foxhole —
    Lightning and thunder above,
    Screaming crash below:
        No joke to keep cool but do.
            Why does her soft voice shake me?

26

Split this throbbing head
    That I may peer in darkness
        To find some answer
            Bright and blue as sun and sky —
                Cheerful omens come today.


What fire is it then
    That some have seen in these eyes,
        This seething fire here
            Even I have had to fear? —
                Uncontrolled it licks the skies.


These black butterflies —
    Is it winter's windy breath
        That turns them to ash
            And buffets them about so?
                Then what burns my soul to ash?

It does my heart good
   To explode in a whirlwind
      Of fire and smoke.
         Her innocence set the spark
           Of joyous conflagration.


What do I do now?
   How do I descend a peak
      That I didn't scale?
         Come my mother! Come O Night!
         Make a star shute to slide down!


Didn't you know it?
   That I and ten thousand men
      Who wouldn't fight for flags,
         Would gladly die for them:
           Those hairs you pluck so freely.

Below our loving,

　　Clean old men hotly discuss

　　　　The ultimate tax.

　　　　　　High in our peaceful tower

　　　　　　　　We kiss amid the gargoyles.

29

Went to a cafe;
  Spent time there expecting you;
    Don't ask me what for.
      A bus glowed like the sunset —
        I left there whistling and happy.


On this brown bottle,
  Yellow and green wax ripples
    Mark a waning night.
      When the sun beams in on me,
        My midnight moon's still waxing.


With a woosh it falls:
  Wick of a once-proud candle
    In a clay jug grave;
      I watch it flicker to death
        Breathing its final fragrance.

30

A snowy dragon —
   The porch roof with icicles
      Hanging from his nose.
         I feel that way too sometimes
            Thinking of my love for you.


Seen through my eyes,
   Death's finger is an icicle,
      And with one "Shhh!"
         He tries to freeze fire and smoke
            Inside my bulging nostrils.


Dread the coming Spring;
   If I feel this listless now,
      What will I do then,
         When Spring's drunkenness stirs me
            To love, as to love it must?

Too many big words!
  If we cut them all in half,
    Rounding the corners,
      Then they wouldn't hurt so much
        When people hit us with them.


Sunspots on my mind:
  What else would blur my vision
    Like these fever fits?
      Even celestial bodies,
        In distant orbits, suffer.


                    Dandelion
Metamorphosis:
  This white puff pausing in flight
    Softly kisses me
      Before becoming yellow bright:
        A flower for your kindness.

## To An Unknown Girl

I know what's real;

Knowing you, I know I know;

For since we spoke once,

I see you in creation

Dancing joyous pirouettes.


Memories of you,

Haunting sentimental halls,

Chill me brushing by.

No one here can hear my calls,

Nor know two ghosts are passing.


Tracing your smoothness

With attentive eyes and hands

I forgive God all,

But gods are petty and proud;

Alone I embrace the wind.

34

My mind invaded

   By fierce and well armed armies

      Of other people;

         I must guard so many gates

            To enjoy my thoughts of you.

35

Though we're surrounded
  By the silent ears of friends
    And other strangers,
      Let's speak of the silences
        That surround our tactful tongues.


            To M. L. K. Jr.
You died that evening,
  And cities burned in your name,
    You the man of love;
      In my midnight dream you said,
        "I know you; I know you all."


          Remember Three Things . . .
Nothing sickens worse
  Than candy coated life pills;
    Don't eat too many.
      The stars are mysterious,
        And beauty lives in your eyes.

You stand there thinking,

    Your fragrant lips half parted,

        Just a kiss away;

            Can your heart be bound against me?

            One step seems like ten thousand.


I'm getting drunker;

    Your lips and eyes sparkle

    In my memory.

        Why you blush and hesitate,

            That's why I'll always love you.


All this empty night

    My drunken sleep is haunted

    By the look you gave:

        Two beautiful burning coals

            That both oceans could not cool.

Midnight and then some . . .
I look under my pillow,
But sleep is not there.
My heart is sad and empty
Like the dumb stare of this page.


"I have a lover;
He writes me glowing poems
On long snowy scrolls;
He praises my downy voice,
And I blush when I meet him."


Everyone loves you
In his own crippled way;
That is your danger:
What we were and have murdered
Shines too brightly in your eyes.

My lips are stamped red
  With the grand official seal
    Of your playfulness.
      I would wear the brand always
        That bound me to you alone.


Her dress is formal,
  Of military fashion;
    She looks soft inside,
      But it strengthens her resolve
        When all the world is warring.


While the silent snow
  Weaves a diamond dream for us
    To blanket our wounds
      And cool our burning souls,
        I need you near me, my love.

39

Atomic nymphs and gods
Converge in laughing wonder
To be your beauty.
In a crowd of multi-grey
I see my lover sparkle.


Like playful tigers,
We stalk each other brushing —
Steel-eyed but warmly.
You share my doubts with me;
Now how can we share our love?

I will not falter,
   Not if you stand beside me;
      Let pettiness play
         Like vicious, vengeful waves;
            They won't wear our love away.



I am comforted;
   Now worldly impermanence
      Seems unimportant;
         Seen in the depths of your eyes,
            The warm eternal darkness.



Sometimes my muscles
   Seem in separate revolt;
      Must maintain order,
         But who am I to dictate?
            Go in peace my children!

41

My shoes are worn out.
   Each ragged leather ripple
      Records my sadness.
         These sad shoes are eloquent,
            But they are not my sole record.


               One Sided Love?
I suppose it's you
   That can say "Thank God it's you,
      This time instead of me." Right?
         Well that's O.K. — I don't mind —
            My face always cracks like this.


               From Vincent
Hey, here is my ear!
   In this clean white envelope;
      I give it to you
         That you may remember me
            And the pain of both of us!

42

I got drunk tonight:
Those red and blue lights flashing
And my bitter mouth.
I can't think straight without you
And can't think when you're around.


At last night's party,
Violence and death fed on
Our conversation,
Like red-eyed hungry spiders.
Are moon and stars still shining?


In my restless sleep,
I dreamt that you awoke me
With kisses so deep
That they burst my swollen heart ...
And I awoke alone and cold.

Choose pine trees and clouds;
    Forget the dusty city;
        Drink deep of the moon.
            Your stomach may be empty
                But better to fill your heart.



If you listen hard,
    You can hear pine trees breathing,
        But not in winter.
            All you can hear in winter
                Is the vacant, icy wind.



Life is pain, is it?
    You know I won't disagree,
        But somehow I think —
            It wouldn't be so bad if . . .
                Like if you and I were we.

45

Pain is an old friend.

    If I feel too complacent,

        I start to worry:

            Like owing six months' rent

                And the landlord stops asking.


              . . . But It Helps

Saturday morning,

    Your scarf waves from the hanger,

        Other traces too;

            You don't have to be around

                To be appreciated . . .


The cold grey ocean —

    If I lose your love, my love,

        I shall be like that:

            In lonely freedom lapping

                The shores of your memory.

Unreachable stars,
   You reflect my saddest eyes,
      You icy fires;
         Nice to have friends like you
            To listen to thoughtlessly.


                  Our Respective Dreams
Bird cries and shadows
   Startle watchful feline senses.
      Through orange curtains;
         Through skies of winter sun,
            We dream of wings and feathers.


I see you kitten,
   Your green iridescent eyes
      Watching spiral wreaths;
         Do you see serpents coiling
            In these harmless smoky swirls?

47

Other men have sung

   To pretty women like you,

      But they were not you.

         No sun shines just like this one —

            None just like the love we make.

48

I am the icing,
  And I am the clear silence
    Of cream covered night.
      Whipped by the winds of Spring,
        I am the gleam on your cheek.


We play with the stars
  Like the children we once were
    When time meant nothing.
      Your mouth still wears the fragrance
        Of the garden and its fruit.


Under a Spring moon,
  This horrid river surges
    Like living oil.
      More than once I jump in fear
        At my echoing footsteps.

49

Sitting by the shore,
    Watching the children swim by,
        I eat an orange.
            High above me was the mound
                Where we sat on Winter snows.


I stare at the dust.
    Playing other people's games
        Wastes what time I have.
            Let me revel with the wind
                Like the castle building clouds.


Up this steep hillside,
    Parched by the Summer sun,
        I stumble with thirst.
            Must I rob these trembling leaves
                Of their refreshing berries?

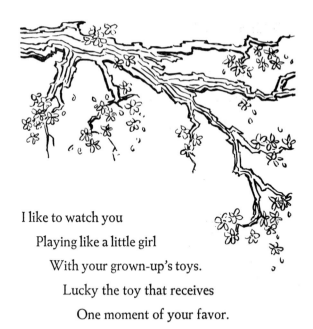

I like to watch you
    Playing like a little girl
        With your grown-up's toys.
            Lucky the toy that receives
                One moment of your favor.


I tell you my love
    At last I know the meaning
        Of "grass for pillow."
            My spirit soars with the clouds,
                But my feet ache with blisters.

51

With crimson flares
    Sparked by the dying sun
        Spring skies are aflame.
            Awed by this texture of life,
                I wait for your silken touch.


As though in a dream,
    I remember last night's storm
        Of thunder and rain,
            The soft warmth of your body
                And the flash across your face.


In a dream palace,
    Long terrace trails of moonlight
        Led me to your side;
            You spoke to me of sadness;
                Now the dawn wakes with our smiles.

## Fin-de-Siècle

Roots cut under me,
　　I'm swept with a swift current;
　　　　Waves swell beneath me —
　　　　　　Broken on some rocky beach,
　　　　　　　　Memories absorbed by sand.


I try to hold on;
　　Knowing my own vanity,
　　　　Vainly I try it.
　　　　　　I am no longer afraid:
　　　　　　　　To let go you must first hold.


Exfoliating,
　　All these universal forms
　　　　Exfoliating:
　　　　　　From the florid namelessness
　　　　　　　　Blossoms and blood and blossoms.

54

Dreamt I wrote a poem

    That freed a boundless spirit;

        Not really so strange

            That it spoke of you alone;

                Takes more than ink to write it.



There are poems there,

    In your walk and face and hair;

        If I could bind them,

            With blood on pulsing paper,

                God would wake from his slumber.



Memories return

    Like melancholy brothers

        When I smell burnt leaves

            On a stranger's jacket:

                That heavy, lonely odor.

Caesar comes, conquers,
　　And squats for ten thousand years,
　　　But for fair lovers —
　　　　One brief glance, one gentle touch
　　　　And for forever . . . longing.


Spring has not yet come,
　　But I, jacketless and blue,
　　　Declare my hot blood.
　　　　Taut against the waning chill,
　　　　I bet on the budding sun.

# INDEX OF FIRST LINES